THE SCIENCE OF GREATNESS

Taking The Guesswork Out of Purpose

KIMBERLY FITTEN

Copyright © 2017 by Kimberly Fitten
Printed in the United States of America
ISBN- 9780578192710
ISBN: 0578192713
Library of Congress Control Number: 2017950867
KS Media and Publishing, Chesapeake, VA

KS Media and Publishing Company
PO Box 459
Cypress, Texas 77410

ACKNOWLEDGEMENTS

I would like to express my gratitude to the many people who supported and pushed me through the journey of writing this book; to all of my friends who talked over, listened, read, offered advice, and gave of your time and expertise to see a friend shine, thank you. To Lorie, Jess, Tracy, Jamesha, Shana, Flora, and Bree, my "Yes" squad; thank you for showing up to the opening of an envelope if it had my name on it! To every student taught, mentored, or reared thank you for teaching me more than I could ever teach you! Your stories empowered and fueled my passion and ultimately my purpose.

I would like to thank Adrienne Bell (AB) for being bold enough to challenge me to believe the world needed to hear what I had to say. Thank you to Pastor Cymaron Dawson and my L.W.K.C family for your love and continued support. Thank you to Marian Coleman for being a remarkable mentor and challenging me to be and do my best. Above all I want to thank my family, the Ducketts, Stubbs, Taylors, and Fittens, who supported and encouraged me at the expense of time away from them. It has been a time consuming whirlwind of a journey and I do not take your selflessness lightly. I love you all.

I would like to thank KS Media and Publishing for the amazing customer service, encouragement, and quality given. What you do is nothing short of amazing! Kyle Kazimour and Ambivalence Studios for the amazing quality and joy you brought to my project! Thank you to Zahra for keeping my life organized and always supporting me. I would like to thank everyone I have met over the years that helped me learn, evolve, and thrive.

Last and not least: Special Thank you to my cousin/sister-friend Ebony Speaks-Hall for every late phone call, helping me process, and praying me back to work. You are an inspiration and I cannot wait for the world to see you shine!

DEDICATION

To my mother for believing and supporting every crazy dream, removing the word "can't" from my vocabulary and teaching me how to fly.

This exciting journey of self-discovery will be a turning point in your life that will empower you to excel and win in every area of your life.

INTRODUCTION

A few years ago, I decided to read a popular book about living life with purpose. Excited to begin my journey I created a social media book club to function as an accountability community and to have a private forum to discuss what we learned. I became a bit frustrated with the lame excuses many of the group members used for not finishing the scheduled readings. They stated they still did not know what to do in order to find their purpose and maybe they were not supposed to do anything other than what they were currently doing. I had no difficulty understanding the concept of purpose, but the book did not tell me how to select the right platform for my purpose, or connect with others to expand my network. It did not tell me how much work living in purpose would require, nor did it enlighten me on the importance of self-assurance. Could purpose be simplified to help anyone understand? Yes! Purpose can absolutely be simplified.

The road to greatness is a systematic journey controlled by the heavens. Think about the best book you've ever read; what was it about the main character that endeared them to you? If the main character was a static character, one that never developed or changed from the beginning to the end of the book, you would have closed the book in the first chapter. When we see a character grow in wisdom and influence it makes us stakeholders in their journey. We love round characters. Round characters are protagonist that experience a cyclical journey where they grow to be better than they were in the beginning of the novel. We are all protagonist in this story called "Life", but our journeys may vary. For example, even though I am an educator I am not called to the same journey as an elementary teacher or college professor because of the variance in demographics we serve. Although we cannot control how our greatness is fashioned, we can understand our journey by embracing every experience that develops OUR character and helps us grow in grace, wisdom, and influence. Throughout this book I will challenge traditional thinking concerning greatness and purpose in order to assist you in achieving the success you deserve.

The following pages will challenge you to stretch beyond areas of discomfort, complacency, doubt, and excuses to access the life you are destined to live, people you are called to reach, and the freedom in knowing what the world needs from you. By the end of this book you will be confident in the greatness within, learn how to connect with people who understand your unique purpose, and most importantly you will be able to confidently define and identify your own purpose. You are and have always been capable of achieving greatness and I am honored to assist you in understanding the science to obtaining greatness and how it can work for you. This exciting journey of self-discovery will be a turning point in your life that will empower you to excel and win in every area of your life.

The path to greatness does not happen with one cataclysmic event that breeds immediate success.

Chapter 1
YOU BELONG CENTER STAGE

There are different stages to greatness. One can compare the journey to greatness to a stage play. There are hundreds of aspects to putting on a play and many positions that need to be filled in order to run a successful production. When the spotlight hits center stage everyone is focused on the actors. The audience is awestruck at the beauty in front of them and no one is thinking about the people working tirelessly backstage to produce a flawless play. Imagine yourself sitting in the audience, you only see the actors hitting their marks, delivering their lines, and looking fabulous; however, it is not your job to wonder how it came to be, it is simply your job to enjoy the production. You do not ponder how long it took the costume designer to make all of the costumes. You do not think about who constructed the stage or who is running all of the technical elements of the show. Even though unacknowledged, all of these positions are necessary in order to produce a memorable work of art. In life, we each play the position of one of the many backstage jobs. We may all want the lead role, but it may not be the right time. The seasons in our lives may call for us to draw the curtains or handle the technical elements, but all of the behind-the-scenes positions help to prepare us for the leading role. Each job is equally important as they equip us for the moments we take center stage. The path to greatness does not happen with one cataclysmic event that breeds immediate success. It is a process that teaches us who we are by challenging our ideas, thoughts, and feelings so we can evolve through what we experience and learn. This is why the path to greatness happens

1

in stages to ensure growth and foster maturity. In order to achieve greatness we must embrace the journey of evolution that lies ahead.

Have you ever felt like you were at the mercy of life? Embracing our journey of evolution allows us to change our perspective and embrace the "why" in what is happening for us and not to us. Embracing these valuable lessons give our experiences meaning and purpose. We do not have to pray for greatness because it is given to us from birth, but we often overlook our inherited ability to be great because of the process. Does achieving greatness take hard work? Yes! A little known fact is that we are all equipped with everything we need to achieve greatness. This ideology is hard for many to accept because society teaches us that people have to be extraordinarily gifted to be memorable. This competitive undertone plants seeds of exclusion in our minds. Seeds of competition, envy, jealousy, anger, frustration, limitations and the like take root and produce a harvest of reasons, excuses and just plain lies of why we are not maximizing our potential.

What excuses have you made to keep yourself from center stage? Have you planted seeds of competition, envy, jealousy, anger and/or frustration that need uprooting? Well, now is your chance to do away with those excuses and take control of your life.

I challenge you to replace all excuses with "I CAN" statements that empower the person you are and will become. The time is now to begin your journey and create a life free from excuses. Use the lines below to explore ways that may be preventing you from taking center stage.

What is preventing me from being center stage?

_____

_____

_____

_____

_____

_____

You have everything you need to collide with greatness.

Chapter 2
UNDERSTANDING YOUR GIFTS

Our DNA is laced with aptitudes, gifts given to us simply for just being born. These gifts assist us in the journey of life, and if we truly embrace them, allow us to collide with greatness. At twenty-two years old, I was working for a major Fortune 500 company sitting in a cubical being paid very well for the little work I was hired to do. Every day I would work, go home and then bar-hop. That was my life, confined to a cubical controlled by mindless 10-key data entry strokes. I participated in office gossip and perpetuated drama, and there was no answer to "how was your day?" because there was nothing to tell. There was no depth, nothing to say and nothing to contribute. One day, while staring at my computer screen it happened, I had an awakening. I realized if I died, at that very moment, the only people who would attend my funeral were the co-workers who actually liked me and those obligated by relation. I had no positive impact on the lives around me, I was not empowering others and I had no legacy to leave behind. The emptiness was palpable and suffocating. I felt like I was drowning in a sea of nothingness. Have you ever felt like you were living life in purgatory? Waiting for something to happen, but you cannot pinpoint what it is that should be happening? The life I was living was absent of accomplishment and far removed from the values instilled in me as a child. I was overcome with a sick feeling accompanied by an all too familiar question "what am I supposed to be doing?" Over time, fear gripped my soul and I began to think about what I was good at. I thought about how I desired to work with children when I was in elementary school and how I envisioned myself as a special education teacher. I also remembered that I enjoyed teaching Sunday school class as well as an infatuation with literature. I decided to go back to school and major in education. I had an epiphany; my greatness was associated with things I was naturally good at. I had to take the time to quiet the noise in my head, sit down, and examine my gifts. What was I celebrated for during my childhood? When did I feel most confident? What did I do without effort? What was I naturally good at that others struggled with? Identifying these gifts gave me access to multiple avenues that would inevitably set me on the path to greatness. Although it is not an exhaustive list, here are my top 20 gifts.

"Kimberly's Top 20 Gifts"

1. Good w/ people
2. Outgoing
3. Charismatic
4. Funny Hilarious
5. Loves to Learn
6. Loves to Teach
7. Articulate
8. Creative
9. Hardworking
10. Athletic
11. Leading
12. Trendy
13. Tenacious
14. Assertive
15. Courageous
16. Caring

17. Writing Poetry
18. Empathy
19. Oration
20. Dancing

Now it's your turn. Gifts are simply things you are good at. Ask your friends, co-workers, and perhaps your social media community what you are naturally good at.

Things to ponder before listing your Gifts:

If someone taught you how to do something, it is a SKILL NOT a GIFT.

Take your feelings out of the equation. Just because you do not like doing something does not mean you are not good at it.

Consider your history. From your childhood to the present, what stories could help you identify areas where you excelled without trying (Lemonade stand, delivering papers).

Be honest with yourself.

As you are creating your list don't over think it. If you cannot list 20 then list 3-5; what matters most is that you become acquainted with what you are naturally good at!

What are you naturally good at?

_____

_____

_____

_____

_____

_____

If you were able to complete your list congratulations! You have just taken time to get to know more about yourself. Revisit this list when you feel discouraged or forget just how talented you are. The reason this exercise was crucial is because I needed you to realize how amazing and unique you are. You have everything you need to collide with greatness. I will let you in on a little secret: this is only the tip of the iceberg; there is so much depth to the greatness inside of you. If you had a little difficulty completing your list, it is ok. Owning this book allows you to connect directly with me. Email me at info@kimberlyfitten.com and I will be happy to help you complete your list!

Passion is the pull, the draw, the need for more and it cannot be confined to a relationship.

Chapter 3
WHAT'S YOUR PASSION?

The first time I heard this word I was in the living room watching television with my mother. There was a couple who had lost their "spark" and the woman exclaimed, "We don't have any passion!" It was then that I was introduced to a skewed understanding of what passion meant. I thought passion was a word that belonged only in truly romantic relationships. However, this perspective changed when I was introduced to cookies n' cream ice cream. As a child, I found myself doing odd jobs to earn money to purchase my new found "passion". How could I be passionate about a dessert the same way the lady on television was passionate about her lover? What was the purpose of this multi-dimensional word? Passion is one of the most misunderstood and subsequently misused word in the English language. Passion is defined as a strong and uncontrollable desire. Passion is never quenched nor satisfied and we oftentimes confuse passion as a synonym for lust completely selling ourselves short. Passion is the pull, the draw, the need for more and it cannot be confined to a relationship. This is why many accuse passion of leaving a relationship when it was never an occupant. Passion is fuel that drives us to keep going when our tanks seem empty. You will need passion in order to achieve greatness.

Passion pushes us to do what we love even when we are exhausted. For example, I could have spent my whole Saturday shopping, but if a friend called and asked me to go with them to another store my answer would be,

"Yes". Why? Because I have a passion for fashion and finding great deals. The excitement compels me to venture out and go beyond how I feel. The things we are passionate about connect to our natural gifting, which in turn leads us to our purpose and on the path to greatness. Before listing my passions, I had to remember that gifts and passions were not the same. Just because I am gifted to write poetry does not mean it is a passion, and if I were tired, I would not push past that to write a haiku. It was equally important for me to identify healthy passions. I love sweets, I am passionate about them, but I often overindulge when I am feeling overwhelmed or ruled by my emotions. I had to be mindful of my unhealthy passions and omit them from my overall list. Here are my top 20 passions:

Kimberly's Top 20 Passions

1. Makeup
2. Pop-Culture
3. Women's Empowerment
4. Helping Others
5. Civil Rights
6. Fashion
7. Hair
8. Vintage Clothing
9. Brainstorming
10. Working-out
11. Singing
12. Exploring New Ideas
13. Healthy Living
14. Mentoring
15. Anything from the 60's
16. Inspiring
17. Painting
18. James Taylor
19. Sweet Treats
20. God

Now it's your turn to list your passions. Just like your gifts, do not be afraid to ask your friends and family what you get excited about or love doing. You may be surprised by their answers and you may discover new passions in the process.

Things to ponder before listing your Passion(s):

You have to absolutely, positively LOVE everything you place on this list.

Even if it is considered a frivolous passion, WRITE IT DOWN!

If you would not do it for FREE it is NOT a passion

Again, if you <u>do not have</u> an uncontrollable drive for it, do not list it!

What are your passions (if you have more than five list the others in the notes section at the end of the chapter)?

_____

_____

_____

_____

_____

_____

If you were able to complete your list congratulations! You have just taken time to get to know more about yourself. Revisit this list when you feel bored or unmotivated. This exercise is important because you need to realize what drives you to excitement. You will need this fuel as a reminder to collide with greatness. If you had a little difficulty completing your list, it is ok. Owning this book allows you to connect with me. Email me at info@kimberlyfitten.com and I will be happy to help you complete your list!

We must confront our weaknesses in order to unlock the purpose that is anxiously awaiting to be pursued.

Chapter 4
WARRIORS & WEAKNESSES

Achilles was a great mythological warrior who was immune to harm because he was dipped in magical water as a baby, however, the only part of his body unprotected was right above his heel because he was dipped head first. He won many battles, but his demise was the great Trojan War where he was killed by a strike to his tendon.. Achilles was not to blame for this unprotected area, it was in a way inherent, however, is there any way he could have guarded his weakness? I am a very candid person, who has not always seasoned my words with diplomacy. It was not what I said that caused people to judge my ability to lead, it was how I said it that made people judge and distance themselves from me. Once I was honest with myself and I addressed that area of weakness people were able to see value in my opinion. This brings us to the third and final list created, my "weakness" list. This list consisted of areas that needed to be improved if I desired to be wildly successful. Did you know that you have had areas of weakness for as long as you have been alive? Think about it. Have you ever gotten in trouble as a kid for making the same mistakes? Did anyone caution you regarding your negative behavior, but you responded "what do they know?" and continued on your merry way? Have your friends politely brought things to your attention, but you still are not open to correction? These things are not just *weaknesses*, they are areas of your personality that need to be refined because they can be detrimental to you colliding with greatness and prospering in your purpose.

Why is it important to embrace and address your weakness list? This list of opportunity areas may block the greatness that awaits you. If you are not mindful of, or refuse to control the areas of your personality that may cause people to be harmed mentally and emotionally, it may stifle your ability to be effective. How can you be great if you are not effective in your sphere of influence? The essence of greatness is the potency of your ability to evoke change. If people would rather avoid you then embrace your greatness will never be reached. When I listed my areas of weakness, I also listed what it would take to overcome them, the antidote. I did not list my weaknesses to constantly remind me of my failures, I listed them so I could also generate a list of ways to self-correct and grow. It is oftentimes easier to claim naivety instead of addressing the issues head on. We must remind ourselves of the remedy for our weaknesses when tempted to succumb to mediocrity. Mediocrity reassures us that our weaknesses are not our fault and that it is easier for others to walk in greatness because they have not experienced what we have. We must confront our weaknesses in order to unlock the purpose that is anxiously awaiting to be pursued. Remember we cannot be amazing without acknowledging our areas of weakness. We live life to the fullest by finding what we love and being nothing short of amazing while doing it. Here is my list of weaknesses and the antidotes.

Kimberly's Weaknesses and the Antidotes

Pride- I remind myself that humility is the currency of life.

Anger- I discipline myself to speak last and listen first

Rejection- I encourage myself to never take anything personal.

Fear of Criticism- I advise myself that feedback is a gift.

Procrastination- I spend every Sunday evening intentionally organizing my week and set reminders on my cell phone to crush my weekly goals.

Fear of Failure- I celebrate every "no" and embrace failure as a learning opportunity.

Prefers working alone- I anticipate opportunities to network; I am one handshake away from a conduit to greatness.

Now it's your turn to list your weaknesses. Just like your gifts and passions, do not be afraid to ask your friends and family what your weaknesses may be. You could be surprised by their answers and may discover areas in your personality that people encounter while engaging with you.

Things to ponder before listing your Weaknesses:

Please be honest with yourself! You may want to refrain from listing these weaknesses because of shame, but even the things you place on this list will assist you on your path to greatness.

YOU can overcome any challenge on your list, therefore there is no need to make excuses.

If you are having issues listing your weaknesses seek input from those closest to you. Resist the urge to be offended by what is said considering this is the last step before we truly take the guesswork out of finding your purpose. Do not take their comments personally, but listen to them and receive all comments with humility.

What are your weaknesses and antidotes?

_____

_____

_____

_____

_____

_____

If you were able to complete your list congratulations! You have just taken time to get to know more about yourself. Revisit this list when you forget the antidotes to your weaknesses. If you had a little difficulty completing your list, it is ok. Owning this book allows you to connect with me. Email me at info@kimberlyfitten.com and I will be happy to help you complete your list!

*The phrase "if only I had…" has been known
to kill thousands of dreams.*

Chapter 5
FEAR CRUSHER

There comes a time in life where the question "why am I here?" is asked. This question is accompanied by a range of emotions: self-doubt, anxiety, self-pity, bitterness, displacement, and FEAR. In actuality these emotions are reasons why we feel we are not worthy of our destiny to be great. Fear simply means to be afraid, but it is an "umbrella' word that holds a gambit of seemingly endless things to be afraid of. There are graveyards full of untapped potential, and the world is full of paralyzed greatness. The phrase "if only I had..." has been known to kill thousands of dreams. Fear is the place we retreat to when faced with the unknown. It is the prison that suffocates our ability to be courageous. Until those fears are confronted, greatness cannot exist and who you truly are cannot be seen. YOU, yes YOU have more than enough to be great; you always have, and it is up to you to access the courage within and live up to your potential.

My mother taught me how to read, write, and count to five hundred before I started kindergarten. I started school reading at a third grade level and was very confident in my academic abilities; however, somewhere along the way I lost that confidence. I was bored by the time I reached middle school and when my mother decided to relocate, I became one of three minorities at my rural high school. My grades plummeted and I graduated 76 out of 89 students in my senior class. I hated school. I was forgotten and no one expected me to excel in anything. I was also told by my counselor that black kids did not learn as well as others, so I should really focus on the things I was good at. They said that singing and acting was what I should do, but I would need to go to college and my grades communicated I was not smart enough.

After high school, I decided to go overseas to teach English as a second language. When I arrived the company that hired me closed down. I was eighteen and homeless on another continent! I secured work at a luxury hotel singing background vocals for American cover bands until I could afford a plane ticket home. Upon returning home my Mother suggested that I apply for a job with a nanny agency, and since I did not have anything better to do I agreed. I was hired immediately as a live-in nanny for the granddaughter of a major retail chain owner in Bryn Mawr, Pennsylvania. One Friday evening she asked me what my life plans were. "Kim, you're really smart, surely you do not plan on watching children for the rest of your life... Villanova is minutes away, and you could take classes while the kids are in school." I told her college was not for me, but my response was conditioned by my conversation with my high school counselor. Fear stood between me and greatness. Had I succumbed to that false reality, I would never have applied to college and would have never made Dean's List or graduated Cum Laude. When I had to defend my graduation project study, my panel of professors told me that I was different. They told me I would change the world and that I was special. These professors put me through hell, but there they were telling me something I had only heard from my Mother. I embraced all that I was in that moment and decided to condition myself to believe what was real, what was inside of me.

We cannot stifle or control how bright our light shines, and our fear can only prolong what we will inevitably embrace. You have two choices: be great or perish from fear. Please stop with all of the excuses of who you are not. Do not allow yourself to believe that your mistakes disqualify you. Whoever hurt you cannot harm your destiny. Whomever you feel is against you is no match for the greatness ahead. You are a fear crusher. You are the only one that can keep you from your destination. Be great or die trying!

What fears need to be crushed in your life?

_____

_____

_____

_____

_____

_____

If you were able to complete your list great job! You have just taken the time to get to know more about yourself. If you had a little difficulty completing your list, it is ok. Owning this book allows you to connect with me. Email me at info@kimberlyfitten.com and I will be happy to help you complete your list!

Greatness is achievable but you must first leave the womb of comfort.

Chapter 6
COMFORT ZONE, DANGER ZONE

Do you know the real reason why babies are born? It is because the life that really matters is outside of the womb. Babies spend nine months in the womb to receive nutrients and develop all of the parts needed to function effectively outside of the womb. The womb is a place of comfort, warmth, and security but if a baby stays too long it can become a place of detriment. If a baby stays in the womb longer than nine months the doctor will suggest immediate removal because it has reached its full state of maturation. When it is time to exit the womb, the baby must vacate the premises willingly or by force. Please do not let the journey ahead frighten you. Greatness is achievable but you must first leave the womb of comfort. There will be times in your journey when you feel like returning to places of comfort, but if you do that you will not experience the levels of greatness that await you. You have grown too big for your comfort zone. It cannot hold all of the greatness you possess, nor can it challenge you to do better.

Each level of greatness calls for bigger faith, greater imagination, deeper dedication, and persistent hard work. DO NOT let your cravings for comfort make you forget the misery and frustration you've experienced that lead you to start your greatness journey. Do not allow nostalgia to make you forget your incredible purpose. Change can be scary, it may be difficult, but the payoff is worth it! When you have outgrown a situation and your gifts have matured and you are supposed to experience something new, you must embrace change to foster the greatness within you. When you refuse change you begin to spew negativity. Change may be intimidating but the push and the stretch pays tremendous dividends. If a shark lives in a pond could it live for long? Would it be able to find sustenance? How long could it live? Sharks belong in the ocean and sea, just like we belong in an endless sea of possibilities. Situations force us to learn patience, learn humility, and gain wisdom. You are a big fish that cannot thrive in small pond. Dare to live life outside of the womb and embrace the possibilities!

Having difficulty exiting your comfort zone? Email me at info@ kimberlyfitten.com and I will be happy to help you pack your bags and leave the comfort zone forever!

What's comfortable about my comfort zone?

_____

_____

_____

_____

_____

_____

You are alive because what happened to you was not enough to break you, and someone needs to hear a story

Chapter 7
THE PURPOSE FORMULA

Purpose is a word that often triggers frustration. This word, full of ambiguity and fear-inducing agents, carries immense weight in which people often run from. Similar to passion, the idea of purpose has been misrepresented and erroneously defined. Purpose has been defined as the reason why we exist. When people gather for a meeting it is for a purpose. When people go to a restaurant it is for a purpose, and when people travel it is for a purpose. Purpose can be compared to a time release capsule, it will always manifest at the right time to assist where it is needed. It is directly correlated to what you love, what you naturally do well, and most importantly your experiences. Our experiences are the catalyst that release purpose.

My Mother was skilled at shielding my siblings and I from the weight of poverty, but there were some things she could not hide. I remember her cooking the last of what was in the kitchen one evening. She'd done her best to stretch what she had for the last two weeks before food assistance was disbursed and there was not enough to feed everyone. My Mother forfeited her portion so my siblings and I could eat, but she told us she wasn't hungry after exerting all of her energy preparing the meal. Later that evening, my brother passed by her room on his way back from the restroom and heard her crying. He came into my room and told me what he'd heard; we both went and sat outside her door, held hands, and with tears streaming down our faces prayed for our mom. I had no intentions of sharing this story with anyone, but during my first year of teaching I found myself trying to motivate a student to take school seriously. They told me there was no point because no one in their family graduated from high school and assuredly stated that this would be their fate as well. The discouraged student told me that I had no idea what it was like to be poor and I needed to stop trying to sell them a dream. Three years later, as I watched her walk across the graduation stage, I suddenly realized that what happened to me was not for me, but it was what she needed to hear in order to have faith to finish what she started. My experiences gave me credibility and allowed me to walk in purpose, the purpose of giving this young lady hope to believe she could achieve more than her current situation. I was stocked with the ability to persuade students they could be more than a teenage parent, a high school dropout, a victim of violence or the afterthought of an absent parent. Each day my purpose afforded me the opportunity to make home visits and give single parents access to family services, as well as mediate conflicts between teachers and students. We cannot fully achieve greatness without embracing the experiences life brings. We often ask why we go through tumultuous times, but those times are not happening to us, they are working for us. Trials and tribulations allow us to build an arsenal of resources to reach others, make an impact, and change lives. Experiences are gifts. Every failure, each disappointment, any trauma, and every win allows us the opportunity to relate, influence, and inspire!

One of the roadblocks to embracing the gift of experience is shame, the idea that somehow we deserved or earned what happened to us. Experiences are difficult to embrace because they are often accompanied by shame. We frequently classify our negative experiences as mistakes, but there are no mistakes. Yes, that's right, THERE ARE NO MISTAKES! There are only decisions, and every decision we make adds to the potency of our greatness. I made the decision to go overseas instead of college, and that decision allowed me to speak a different language, learn from other cultures, and mature in ways I will never forget. I also experienced many dangers that reminded me of what I was made of and how I was equipped with the tenacity needed to endure life's hardships. These decisions, not mistakes, opened my eyes to see who I really was and what I could truly accomplish in the best and worst of times. Shift your paradigm and acknowledge the opportunities in your story.

Many find it hard to embrace negative experiences because pain is viewed as something that victimizes us instead of using it as a stepping-stone to catapult us to purpose. We often allow ourselves to wallow in self-pity as to why we are unable to achieve success in life. I encountered a single mother in her forties complaining about the quality of her life. She had four children, never married, and hated her job. She admitted she was short-tempered, impatient, unforgiving, and bitter. However, when I asked her what she'd done in her 40+ years to live a better life, she replied by placing blame on her father who left in her adolescent years, the trauma of her sexual assault, having to raise her children on her own, and people at her job who want to see her fail. She took no ownership and placed blame on everyone else. Does this sound familiar? Does this hit home? Is this you?

I am a survivor of sexual assault, but had I not transitioned from a victim to a survivor I would have used the experience as a reason why I did not achieve greatness. Even though what they did to me was wrong, I could not adopt the belief that this excused me from living a life full of purpose. There are women all over the world who made the choice to get counseling, who made the choice to be a survivor and not a victim, who made the choice to take their power back and create a safe space for others who would experience the same thing. They are thriving in life. They refused to die from the experience, therefore, giving them control over how long they allowed their negative experiences to rule their lives. The hard reality is that nothing we experience is 100% responsible for our quality of life. Using events that occurred in our childhood as an excuse is irreverent of the gift, the opportunity of being alive. Life is the most precious gift we will ever receive, and we must ask ourselves if we want to spend it in victim, survival, or thrive mode. I know what it is like to be the victim. I have experienced rape, molestation, homelessness, illness, unemployment, adolescent trauma, physical abuse, and religious mental abuse. Regardless of my painful experiences, I walk in greatness because I use these life lessons to give hope and breathe life into others who do not yet see the light at the end of the tunnel. ALL things, the good, the bad, the ugly work in collaboration to produce goodness for us. Making the decision to use what we have been through does not exonerate those who have wronged us, but frees us from the subjugation of their actions. You are alive because what happened to you was not enough to break you, and someone needs to hear a story of not only survival, but also someone who thrived in the face of adversity. It is okay to decide enough is enough, and take your power back from the situation and chose to live.

Right now you are probably thinking "Ok Kim, I know what my gifts, passions, weaknesses, and experiences are but what is my purpose? How do I find it?"So let's work on finding the answers to your questions. Add your aptitudes to your passions and then multiply the sum by your purpose, divide that product by your experiences and this will equal greatness.

Purpose [(Aptitudes + Passion) ÷ Experiences] = Greatness. I have a natural aptitude to teach and I add that to my passion for mentoring; I then divide that by my experience of growing up poor and multiply it by my purpose to reach those who are experiencing the same thing, but need to know they can overcome poverty to equal greatness. Your purpose is always making others better by giving hope, clarity, strategies, tips, and wisdom. Your purpose is everything you have been through. Using every gift, passion, and experience to reach people that are currently going through what you have experienced and survived. I revisit my gifts, passions, and experiences to devise innovative fresh ways to give hope. There are women who have experienced sexual assault and questioned if they would ever be whole again. I use my similar experience, my gift of empathy and my passion to strengthen them at their lowest points. I not only share my experience, but stand as a real-life example of not only the ability to survive but thrive. I will use my list of gifts and passions to fill in a few equations so you can see how it works.

> Purpose- to help/reach others (teach + women's empower-ment/vintage clothing/shopping on a budget) ÷ not having proper clothes= showing women how to look their best on a budget to build self-esteem.
>
> Purpose- to help/reach others (writing + singing) ÷ I wrote songs in my childhood as a form of therapy = creating a songwriter's therapy program for children who experience trauma.

Notice that I placed more than one passion in the first equation because that is what it took to produce the desired outcome. Our purpose never changes. We are meant to assist others, but how we assist them is up to us, and greatness is experienced through each outcome. What passion, gift, and experience will you use to continually make those around you better?

You can never be great unless you are doing something for others. How will your greatness benefit the world? If you are not perpetuating hope, then you are not walking in your purpose.

Now, it's your turn to work this equation out on your own. What have you experienced that allows you to relate to others? Have you been addicted to something? Have you experienced heartbreak, divorce, in-fertility, child abuse, loss of a loved one, success in business, weight loss... etc.? Fill in your equation and start there. Remember, purpose evolves in order for us to experience new levels of greatness. You may want to complete the equation multiple times, please use the notes sections to generate more ideas. Revisit this equation when you feel stagnate, bored, or underwhelmed.

My Purpose[(____ + ____) ÷ Experiences] = Greatness

If you were able to complete your purpose formula great job! If you had a little difficulty completing the formula, it is ok. Owning this book allows you to connect with me. Email me at info@kimberlyfit-ten.com and I will be happy to help you solve your purpose equation!

Thoughts about my purpose formula(s):

My Purpose Formula #1

My Purpose [(___ + ____) ÷ Experiences] = Greatness

My Purpose Formula #2

My Purpose [(___ + ____) ÷ Experiences] = Greatness

_____

_____

_____

_____

_____

_____

Your platform is the "magic" feather,
but your purpose will work anywhere.

Chapter 8
PLATFORM VS. PURPOSE

Dumbo was one of the most annoying movies I was forced to watch. I never understood why a movie with singing crows became so popular, furthermore, an elephant with big ears is not abnormal. Dumbo was born with ears bigger than all of the other circus elephants and his mother protected him from the negative words of others. One day, his mother was locked away after trying to protect her son from a circus spectator. Unfortunately, without his mother to protect him, Dumbo was faced with the brutal reality of what others thought of him. He began to curse the fact that he did not blend in with his peers. He later meets Timothy Mouse who gives him a "magic" feather convincing Dumbo it will help him fly and become the main circus attraction. During a show Dumbo ends up in a life or death situation without his magic feather; he feels helpless and almost gives up until Timothy Mouse tells him the feather was only a trick to make him comfortable with flying because he did not believe in himself. Once Dumbo realized the feather was a prop, he frees himself from the opinions of the other elephants, and the shame of his big ears. Why did I use this extended metaphor? It is quite simple. Your platform is the "magic" feather, but your purpose will work anywhere.

The average adult changes jobs a minimum of seven times in a lifetime. Have you applied for a job or promotion in your company thinking you were seeking purpose? Are you sure your purpose is connected to your job? Just because we experience moments of promotion does not mean we

31

are working in our purpose. Many of us limit our sphere of influence by pigeonholing ourselves to fulfill the same role day in and day out. Why? Because we negate to differentiate platform from purpose. Purpose is the way we affect the world, and platform is the conduit by which we display our purpose. Platforms give us the opportunity to showcase our purpose for a specific audience that may require our expertise. When I was a classroom teacher I believed my purpose was to reach the children I taught, and I never imagined being effective outside of the classroom. I was in my comfort zone and doing something different frightened me. When I left the comfort of my classroom, I was afforded the opportunity to expand my sphere of influence to reach parents, siblings, grandparents, and my community. I now have a weekly broadcast and podcast that expands my purpose and accesses thousands of people, but I first had to release the "magic" feather and understand that I was born with an extraordinary purpose that does not need a prop to shine. I am an educator, mentor, coach, and author;however, had I confined myself to the classroom I would have missed functioning in my full purpose and the magic of utilizing multiple platforms. Are you using your current platform as a security blanket? Are you holding on to that dead-end job out of fear? Are you using your children as an excuse to avoid change? Are you staying in a relationship that no longer serves you? You were meant to fly and you cannot spread your wings holding on to your feather. Let your purpose lead the way and open your mind to the possibility that you may need to change your platform today! Now that you are on the path to discovering your full purpose, you must also be sensitive to opportunities to shift your platform because it will give your purpose maximum impact.

What platform will you use to serve your purpose?

_____

_____

_____

_____

_____

_____

If you are having trouble identifying what platform will best serve your purpose, it is ok.   Email me at info@kimberlyfitten.com and I will be happy to help you discover the platform where you will dominate and prosper!

More thoughts about my platform(s)...

_____

_____

_____

_____

_____

_____

Purpose killers are unassuming and if we do not shore up our defenses, they could limit our ability to be effective.

Chapter 9
PURPOSE KILLERS *3 THINGS TO AVOID AT ALL COST*

Knowing your purpose is an empowering feeling all humans desire to experience. There is an assurance one has when they know what they are purposed to do and walk in that purpose. However, there are three purpose killers that can cause us to become stagnant and ineffective if we are not mindful of them. Purpose killers are unassuming and if we do not shore up our defenses, they could limit our ability to be effective.

Purpose Killer #1- Loss of Imagination
I had the most amazing childhood full of whimsical wonderment. My Mother would help us build forts with sheets covered in stars, connect it to a fan and place books around the edges so the air would lift it and make a magical sphere of youthful mischief. We would pretend we were the Hubble Spacecraft exploring the depths of the unknown to save the world and discover uncharted territories. This gift of imagination gave me ambition to start my own newspaper, delegate responsibilities to my siblings, and finish a publication everyday for my Mother to read. Imagination made each day an adventure and forced me to expand my mind to have imaginary interviews with Oprah, give acceptance speeches for awards, and choreograph dance routines. Imagination

eliminated the limits, freed my dreams from the confines of conventional thinking, and gave me the ability to THINK BIG. I still utilize my imagination for my purpose because it allows me to brainstorm an idea, believe it can be done, set goals, and crush them. Imagination eliminates doubt and fear and we need it to fuel our creativity. When we eliminate imagination we welcome fear and doubt. We add phrases like "it can't be done" and "this will never work" into our vocabulary and ultimately allow it to slowly kill our purpose. Purpose is attractive when it is packaged in ingenuity. There are many people who have experienced the same situations. There are many people who have the same gifts and passions, but the differences in how they display them demands attention. Imagination is the key to discovering platform and developing fresh ideas to strategize how we will help others. You must embrace thinking big and unleash your imagination!

Purpose killer #2- Negative Thinking/Talk

I became extremely annoyed when my Mother would tell me that I could not do something. I would often plead my case giving her all of the reasons why it was beneficial for me to do what I was asking her permission to do. We did not like when our parents told us what we could or could not do, but for some reason, as adults, we consistently limit ourselves by using the word CAN'T. Even when we make our own rules and set our own limits we still doubt our abilities and perpetuate negative limitations. How many times have you talked yourself out of doing something great? How many times have you refrained from speaking up or pursuing a great idea because you second-guessed your ability? This negativity is a purpose killer. If you do not believe in yourself, no one else will! When you say you cannot do something the Universe hears you. The Universe is unable to discern sarcasm and the power of the spoken word is very real. When you say you will never be successful, you do not have the knowledge, you are too fat, too skinny, not good enough, not likeable you make it a reality. What you speak will manifest and it is your responsibility to speak positively about yourself at ALL times!

Think of yourself as a precious commodity, you cannot expect others to buy-in and invest if you are not invested in who you are and your abilities. Just because what you are purposed to do may be out of your comfort zone does not mean you are not capable and ill equipped to do it. You are unequivocally exceptional and your value is positively immeasurable. If you do not believe you are good enough no one will ever experience the greatness in you. You must hold your head high and believe that you are destined to achieve greatness and your presence commands success.

Purpose Killer #3- People's Opinions

There is a difference between opinion and constructive criticism. Constructive criticism is merited and the person giving it is credible. Opinions are subjective in nature and have no suggestions on how to better the situation. When I submitted my PhD proposal, my committee chairs told me my submission was subpar and beneath the doctoral committee standards. They then pointed out every area that needed to be addressed and a checklist of things needed to be done in order to enhance my work and move on in the program. Even though their critique was harsh, it was accompanied by suggestions to make me better. Opinions are of no use without a checklist of how to make things better. If someone is telling you what you cannot do or who you will never be that is their opinion. If you surround yourself with opinion-filled people they will crush your spirit and suffocate your purpose. People who speak negatively about your purpose have not checked into their own purpose or allowed the negative talk of others to cause them to let go of their dreams. Guard your ear-gates and do not allow pessimistic people to kill your purpose softly with their songs of negativity.

You must constantly ask yourself what are the places inside of you that prefer negativity, lack of imagination, and opinions to creative positivity? Avoid these purpose killers and continue to walk in your purpose with your head held high. Greatness awaits and you never have to dignify negativity with a response.

What and/or who are my purpose killers?

_____

_____

_____

_____

_____

_____

If you were able to identify your purpose killers great job! If you had a little difficulty, it is ok. Email me at info@kimberlyfitten.com and I will be happy to help you annihilate your purpose killers!

Your greatness is directly correlated to the people you surround yourself with.

Chapter 10
BUILDING YOUR TRIBE

No matter how great you are, no matter what you are purposed to do, no one can be great on their own. Connecting with like-minded people propel us to higher levels of greatness. Surrounding ourselves with the right people allows us to create a super product. We can generate our own ideas, however, there is a synergy created when people with the same goal join forces. As a child, my brother was a superhero fanatic, and whatever he loved, I loved because he was my best friend. Saturday morning cartoons was our favorite time because we could watch our favorite cartoon Voltron. Voltron formed when five separate team members interlocked and combined their forces to create a super machine to defend the universe. When the situation proved too much for one team member to handle on their own, they enlisted the assistance of the rest of the team to complete the mission. Art imitates life. We all have a purpose on our own, but there is something to be said about what is created when like-minded people are on the same team. It can ultimately save the world. We will need others to assist us on our greatness journey. That is why building a purpose tribe is important. A purpose tribe must consist of positive thinkers who are visionaries and creative, enterprising individuals who can bring the best out of a seemingly impossible situation. When you create a network of people who are passionate about their purpose, the sky is your limit. The members of your tribe must increase your effectiveness. A tribe should consist of people who want the best for you, themselves, the local community, and the world at large. Every member of your tribe serves a unique role.

The Encourager- This is the first person you call when you need to be reminded why you are doing what you are doing. They are the eternal optimist no matter the circumstance and their optimism breeds solutions. They get joy out of keeping others hopeful. You need as many encouragers as possible.

The Promoter- They will not only show up to the opening of an envelope, they will create the invitation, mail it, and compel others to support. They can be found informing others of positive events and people to connect with in the community. They do not do it for recognition, instead, they are rewarded by simply sharing the information.

The Judge- This person looks at an idea/situation/event to analyze and assess the plans for possible areas of improvement. They are all about the bottom line and assessing areas of potential opposition. Their honest feedback is greatly valued and if utilized correctly can save you time, money, and disappointment. They love to see you succeed and they count it a joy to look out for your best interest.

The Wisdom Wizard- You may become annoyed that they are always right, but you would never think about starting a project without seeking their advice. This person is very successful and has a well-rounded amount of life experience. This mentor or advisor tells you what you need to hear and not what you *want* to hear. Their wisdom keeps you from making decisions that could keep you from achieving success. Their only desire is to help you avoid their pitfalls and see you win.

The Collaborator- This person loves to join forces and create. They specialize in generating ideas, assist in the planning and implementation process, and when your project is completed, they will ask you to return the favor. They keep the circle of positive support in rotation because they believe in paying it forward and the positive changes created when working with others.

The Ace- This person has a complementary skill set to make up for your areas of weakness. They know you and want the best for you and they can often be found smoothing out the rough edges. They have a knack for knowing how to finesse a situation when you are unable to, and they often serve as your public relations expert.

When we surround ourselves with positive people, our productivity dramatically increases. When we see our tribe members successful, thriving, and making an impact it compels us to work harder to achieve or exceed those same goals. The right tribe motivates us to push a little harder and admonishes us to remain humble through accountability. They do not let us remain stagnant and unproductive. They remind us of who we are and what we are called to accomplish. Are you surrounded by people that push you? Are you surrounded by positive people? Are you connected to achievers and optimists? Your greatness is directly correlated to the people you surround yourself with. If you surround yourself with negativity and mediocrity, do not be surprised when your altitude is limited. Dismiss the people in your life who can only remind you of the negative and never encourage or push you to your potential. You must select people who crave to see others winning and achieving greatness. Surround yourself with purpose junkies! If you want to create synergy and see your community change, start building your purpose tribe.

Have you discovered your Ace and Collaborator? Did your Encourager or Promoter come to mind? Is it possible that your Judge or Wisdom Wizard needs to be identified? It's time to build your tribe or engage the one you have with your newly discovered purpose formula.

Who is in my purpose tribe?

_____

_____

_____

_____

_____

_____

If you were able to identify your purpose tribe excellent job! Need a tribe? Join my Purpose Junkies Private Facebook Group. Email me at info@kimberlyfitten.com and I will be happy connect with your purpose tribe!

Humility is like a multivitamin, everyone needs
a dose to maintain stability.

Chapter 11
HUMILITY IS YOUR SUPERPOWER

Clark Kent worked at the Daily Planet as a News Reporter. He fetched coffee, ran errands, endured constant berating from his boss, and was friend-zoned by the girl he loved because he was a timid, horned-glasses wearing geek from Smallville, Kansas. However, whenever the city of Metropolis needed him, he would find the nearest dark corner and change into the world's beloved "Superman". He had numerous super powers. He had x-ray vision, he could fly, he had super strength, he had eyes that could double as a heat-searing ray, he could blow cold air and freeze anything, he had super speed and was unstoppable to all things except Kryptonite. Lois Lane, the woman he loved, was desperately in love with Superman, but would never give Clark a second glance. Even though he could have gained popularity, fame, and wealth he never revealed who he was and kept his super alter ego in check. He could have had the woman of his dreams and he could have crushed his boss with his pinky finger for berating him, but he put a harness on his powers instead. He decided to remain humble because he knew that behaving in a braggadocios manner could jeopardize the safety of the world. He never demanded gratefulness from the people of Metropolis, nor did he never use what he did for others as a bargaining chip or leverage. He helped others because it was what he was born, equipped, and purposed to do.

Humility is like a multivitamin, everyone needs a dose to maintain stability. Humility reminds us not to think too highly of ourselves and to consider the vital role grace plays in our achievement of greatness. When we experience levels of greatness, we also experience pride in what we have accomplished. It is quite easy to forget our humble beginnings while celebrating our achievements. There are some who would prefer their small beginnings to stay in the past, but the ones who are wise revisit those small beginnings to serve as a motivator and reminder of how blessed they truly are. Humility is our superpower. It gives us access to platforms beyond our dreams because we do not count it as something we are entitled to but rather something we have be graced to do. When we believe WE are great we start using "I" statements: I changed their life, I built this company, I landed this client. I statements make us delusional by thinking we achieved greatness on our own, and we can quickly become self-serving and self-promoting. There are so many talented people in the world with so much to give and every day others are born to achieve greater than those before them. You must remember just how fortunate you are and that it is an honor to serve the human race. It is through humility that you gain favor and admiration of people in high places. Obtaining favor is not why you help others, or why you remain humble, but it is a byproduct of humility.

Humility says "I made it and YOU can make it too!" We do not lose anything by helping others and continuing to offer our services. Bill and Melinda Gates, Oprah Winfrey and Mark Zuckerberg often use their platform to promote humility and giving back to others. These power brokers could easily set the world on fire with irrational ideas with their strong media and technological influence, but they instead choose to ignite the world with compassion. Confidence is indeed key, but humility is the multivitamin that should be consumed and absorbed by all on a daily basis.

Need a small dose of humility? Email me at info@kimberlyfitten. com and I will be happy to help you access this purpose-enhancing super power!

In what ways can I activate humility as my greatness super power?

_____

_____

_____

_____

_____

_____

*Greatness is not only what you do,
but what you compel others to do!*

Chapter 12
PAY IT FORWARD

Now that I have shared with you how gifts, passions, weaknesses and experiences breed greatness, I must inform you of the most vital component to achieving greatness. We achieve relevance by the seeds we sow and the ground we cultivate. We sow daily with the understanding that we may never get to see our harvest because we plant with vision for the generations that do not yet exist. As an educator I believed I was paying it forward, but I was getting paid for what I was doing, so I was not giving back at the level my purpose required. I continued to see a need in my community that could not be met within the confines of my eight-hour day and something needed to be done. From time to time I would purchase meals for students, but that was a quick-fix with no sustainability. I eventually had to ask myself where was I needed? I decided to start my own organization dedicated to mentoring young women in the area of vision and success. We created vision boards, engaged in community service projects, peer mentoring programs, and high expectations of self-respect. The feedback was phenomenal and the feeling of accomplishment that accompanied the feedback was positively overwhelming. It was then that I experienced my first collision with greatness. A few of the young ladies participating in the mentorship program desired to share what they've learned with individuals in their sphere of influence. They began to speak with their peers in the hallways and during lunch, in their churches and at community events, spreading the importance of having vision and self-respect. It was then I realized that what I planted not only harvested but reproduced. Greatness is not only what you do, but what you compel others to do! I am unable to achieve greatness through my own accomplishments because I have a limited reach, however, by paying it forward I create an endless, unlimited chain reaction of hope that knows no boundaries. I also created a social media vlog dedicated to inspiring and encouraging others to walk in their greatness. This is another example of paying it forward because the message can be digested and shared with people I may never meet, but have access to life-changing, greatness-enhancing strategies. Paying it forward is not limited to monetary giving, it is literally giving of yourself. What you know and what you have experienced is enough to transform the world! There is someone waiting to be mentored by you. Someone needs to hear your story, so they can believe that their success is possible. There is someone who needs your wisdom to avoid the pitfalls you've experienced in order to be great. Why would you want to be selfish and keep your expertise from the world? The world needs what you have to offer. Where can you volunteer? Where are you needed? How will you meet the need? Your influence is necessary, and I implore you to put it to work today!

Need help with strategies to pay it forward or starting your own non-profit organization? Email me at info@kimberlyfitten.com and I will be happy to help you transform your community!

How will I pay it forward today?

_____

_____

_____

_____

_____

_____

JUST ONE MORE THING...

My home is filled with books purchased over the years, sometimes I re-read them, but for the most part they take up space and serve as decorative pieces. There are a select few that go wherever I go, and I reference them much like a cookbook because they hold the recipes of life. I re-read them when I feel I have lost my way or need to be reminded of what I must accomplish. These books look much different than the ones used as decorative pieces. Knowing your purpose and walking in it daily is an extraordinary gift that gives life new meaning. It is even more extraordinary when you share what you have learned with others who find themselves asking the same questions that convinced you to purchase this book. Remember how you felt before finding and or revisiting your gifts, passions, weaknesses, and experiences? Remember the frustration you experienced when you did not have an answer to what your purpose was? I remember those feelings and they compelled me to share *The Science of Greatness* with you. I would like you to do the same by sharing what you have learned and experienced with others. Any life-changing book I have read I made sure to purchase another copy for someone I knew needed it just as much as I did. I implore you to obtain a copy for someone else. Start a book club or share it with your youth group, but whatever you do PLEASE share this powerful, universal message. Discovering purpose and achieving greatness is not a suggestion but a social responsibility.

If you or someone you know needs to discover purpose and experience the joys of greatness email me at info@kimberlyfitten.com or visit www.kimberlyfitten.com

93241849R00037

Made in the USA
Columbia, SC
10 April 2018